KAI'LA LAKHAI

Copyright © 2024 by By Chef Khonsu

All rights reserved. No part of this book may be reproduced in any manner whatsoever without written permission except in the case of brief quotations embodied in critical articles and reviews.

First Printing, 2024

Kai'la LaKhai

A Poetic Anthology Of Life's Transitions

BY CHEF KHONSU

*Illustration's By Ariana Radcliffe,
Tyson Marzouq, Ty-Quasia Rippey,
Yvonne Triche*

GoldJestic

Chapter 1

Kai'la LaKhai

To beings freeing themselves.
Thank you earth for all you've expressed.

Note From Khonsu

The only thing consistent is change.
The transition can be tedious, sometimes I refuse to take it.
Instead I'd rather rock back and forth, looking at the view from the cliff of the old me. Just looking at what I want... What I dream. What I want to reach.
Why?...
When I can just fall right into place.
To fall and float in the abyss of self and that endless river I'm paddling. Where I can build known cities of my own life.
It's mine right?
I know the fall will be full of cycles and abundant lessons. Revealing masks that will uncover and unveil my true being.
I will stand and see I'm exactly where I need to be.
Choosing me.

I gift this book to you.
I kept feeling it's something more. I gift you this book to show we all are figuring it out. Whether we are man or woman or both in between. We are human. We are set to be on this earth to solely be ourselves and free to choose ourselves authentically. Each and everyone of us are galaxies conquering our forever. This book holds my vulnerability. Some things most don't see in humans these days. Some things we need to see, and hear and acknowledge. I want to express it's okay. Everything we are is the equation of self, even though each equation is different the sum always equals beauty. Blossom to be that. Choose to be your best so you won't disappoint yourself. It's that simple.

With Love and Truth ,
LaKhai K. Sunsword
Kai'la K. Marion

* Accept or Reject - 9
* 7/6/22 - 10
* 7/9/22 - 11
* Damn Grass - 12
* Folding Chair - 14
* 7/7/22 - 16
* Free Thing - 17
* What's The Point - 18
* 11/10/21 9:55pm - 19
* 11/10/21 10:00pm - 20
* Self Sufferring - 21
* Consistency - 22
* Illusional - 23
* Ego Death - 25
* Mind Yours - 26
* Within - 27
* Stagnant - 28
* 7/28/22 - 29
* 8:32pm - 31
* Pretty - 32
* Still Mirror - 33

* Do - 34
* 7/22/2012 - 35
* 9/4/2012 - 36
* 12/12/2017 - 37
* 2/9/2018 - 38
* 03/22/2018 - 39
* Roots - 40
* See You Later - 41
* Upside Down - 42
* 02/02/16 - 44
* 02/23/16 - 46
* 06/9/2016 - 47
* BBB - 48
* 11/10/2017 - 49
* 02/17/2017 - 50
* 02/21/17 - 51
* 03/31/2017 - 52
* Senseless - 53
* 11/02/2017 - 54
* 11/1/2017 - 55
* Choice - 56

* Honesty - 57
* 03/03/2018 - 58
* 09/17/2018 - 59
* Mantra - 61
* Momma - 62
* 8:07pm - 63
* Live Nightmares - 64
* 8:31 Am - 65
* Who Is She - 66
* 4:04 Pm - 67
* Reciprocate - 68
* Forever Maybe - 69
* Spicy - 70
* Happy - 71
* He /She - 73
* Big Little Bro - 74
* Parents - 76
* Toxic Love - 78
* Hierarchy - 79
* Love Not Need - 80
* Factual - 81

* Reminder - 82
* Placement - 83
* Her And I - 84
* Reality - 86
* Relax - 88
* 7:49 Pm - 89
* Earth/Wind/Fire - 90
* Soul Food - 91
* Four Walls - 92
* 11:56 Pm - 93
* Self Made Prison - 95
* Chained Loose - 96
* 1:28 Pm - 97
* First Off - 98
* Space - 99
* Circle Back - 100
* T For Tea - 102
* 10:09 Am - 106

* Just Me - 107
* Break - 108
* Pointy Heart - 109
* Kaila LaKhai - 112

8 ~ BY CHEF KHONSU

Ty - Quasia Rippey

Accept or Reject

She was frail
Not much to spare
One more push and she faded into the endless bay of anxiety
Her girlfriend can even see the void of lifeless urgency
to just feel again
After all
her life did just transform into a shift of demons
She still had the mind of who she truly was
but the shadows were there and her ego death was not
And in order to set free
She must die
be free of what saddens her
to either accept or reject
The being of her own responsibility
7/2/22

7/6/22

What does not lie
lays between conscious and flesh
The feeling of loneliness
right after the smile of success
Love forms happiness
till choices create locked doors
and insecurities become shame
and shame becomes insanity
All from one check point of emotion
drowning
not really aware
to just stand up
And be the flesh of consciousness
6:12 am

7/9/22

Shoulder high
Neck in pain
Over thinking
Finding my pace
Realization of doing too much
But feeling so limitless to the sky above
Fatigue from others
Not breathing much
Caring for others
Not self
Time is needed for that
5:25 pm

Damn grass

Green tones of her rooting
She is all i tend to let go
Sitting with her smoking
Instead of Flowing
instead Growing
Not a dark place
but not a sight
She's always calling me in the midst of emotion
Whispering to stay in the circle
Knowing it's just a circle
While everything changes out field
I am capable of just this stance
I am more then just this grass
The grass is greenest where you plant your roots
And my seeds are each step i choose
So for now mary jane
Let's break away to another spot
Where change is the only thing consistent
And life is more
Is more then
This damn grass

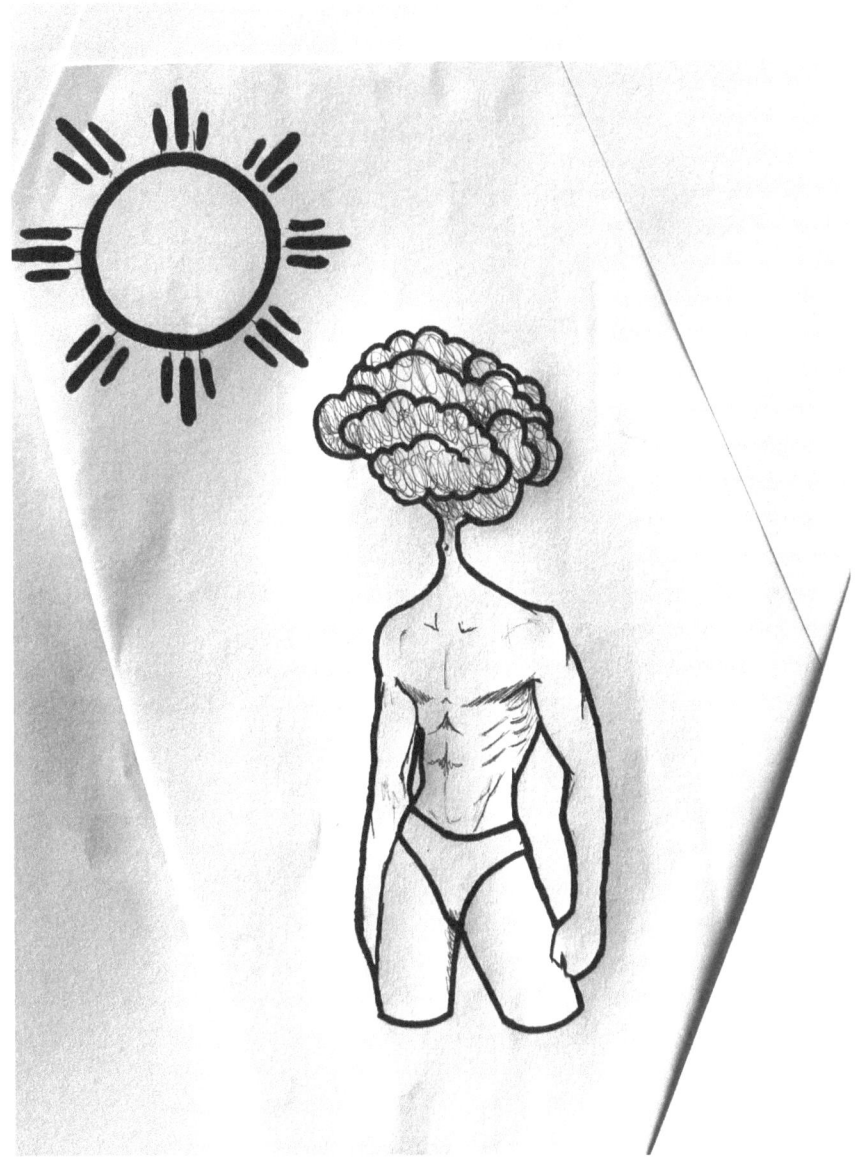

Ty - Quasia Rippey

Folding Chair

He always holds one thing back
If it's about him
It's gonna be about him
One thing I love about him is just that
He is a simple man who happens to be gay
but selfish as he should
He always comes to me after things are done
expressing thoughts after things are settled
He is a gay man
The finest you can see
Tall
Handsome
A perfect fit to grab the eye
But what's out loud is not spoken internally
He was battling himself with his securities
seeing other men define differently
He is a man of his element
a man of his work
Clean
dedicated
always making sure he is good
Not saying gender or sexuality defines your responsibility
because it doesn't
I'm stating this because men like to follow
And if the lead isn't acknowledging
they seem to fold
And the only thing you can do with a folding chair
is put it back in storage
till you need it again
to sit

For just a minute
and the cycle repeats
What gets me about men is how intelligent one can be
but how easily they can become a folding chair
simply because ones being
is being
without letting another being be

7/7/22

Being present
Taking it step by step
Conscience of my triggers
Unaware of forward actions
In a void
Confused
Sad
Can't move
Trying to pull out of the familiar
knowing the familiar
is home to my comfort.

Free Thing

Depression
Able to sit in my sorrows
Nothing else matters but the worse things
Everything is for the worse
But depression
It ..it gets old
And hatred can only be sold
So this free thing
called breathing
Maybe just that feeling

What's the point

I don't get it
What's the point
How can i love on insecurities thats none of my own
How can i genuinely love and not get half in return
Gravity doesn't ask
It just do
My fucking life is blooming like a fucking cacoon
Letting go of this hibernation is so fucking new
But i gotta move
And be love
Because
I am the point

11/10/21

I feel it in my body
The way you make me feel
Up and down emotions
Life shouldn't be as crazy as this frenzied roller coaster
Gotta just breathe
Gotta just be
Aint no fucker like me
I am creativity
I am me
9:55 pm

11/10/21

I will never understand the ground your feet land
The vision you planned
I will never understand
And it's not my place
Rather my choice
To choose to be whole
And be in my own peace
10:00pm

Self Suffering

Oooooouuuaaaahhhhhhh !
People make me mad
But I let them

Consistency

It's the small details that creates a situation into its outcome
Self investments is nice
But when you have to say no to the comfortability of self destruction
The shit gets real
Keep going
It's a beautiful day
Fear is the core
Pull back of consistent movement
Invest in self
Protect myself

illusional

Comfortability has to be protected
Insecurities must be heard
If not
Voices are louder than actions
And actions are not equal than words
Scenarios of vibrations approaches
Collapsing reality
Closing all doors to sanity
Losing control
While I look back at you
In disbelief
Wow..
Illusional

Arianna Radcliffe

Ego Death

I'm no longer walking to my moms house
I am walking to that road where all my feelings are exposed
to the very tip of the cliff of death
To fall to my true self

Mind Yours

The structure of my mind can never compare to yours
The structure of my soul can never be built like yours
Mind your own
Accomplish more

Within

The day you shatter and reconstruct
Is the day your growth cannot be touched
Beauty has no wrong
Beauty has no sight
Understand that beauty comes within your light

Stagnant

Loneliness is not a grudge to hold
Dark and consistent
It feels illegitimate
I know a step out can change
I know just a try can feel less restrained
But fuck that
I wanna be stuck here...
In my sorrow
It's not like anyone twitches
from seeing my skin and stitches
Only when the end is near
Or the high is high
I see I am not so lonely
But
That's honestly a lie
Because when I step out
From that consistent sadness
My energy shifts
It was right under my stubbornness
To smile and change

7/28/22

Its that day of the week
Where I stab myself in the ass
again
Some say Trans is a weakness
Some ask when am I done with the syringes
Rather less there shouldn't be confusion
Gender is so important to these beings
When in all actuality
We are just like the three consistent energies
Sun
Moon
Water
You know
The Masculine
The Feminine
And the flow of the two
I am not the needle
Or the bottle of my secured super powers
I am just truly
Setting free
Showing thee
Anything is anything
And I am me

30 ~ BY CHEF KHONSU

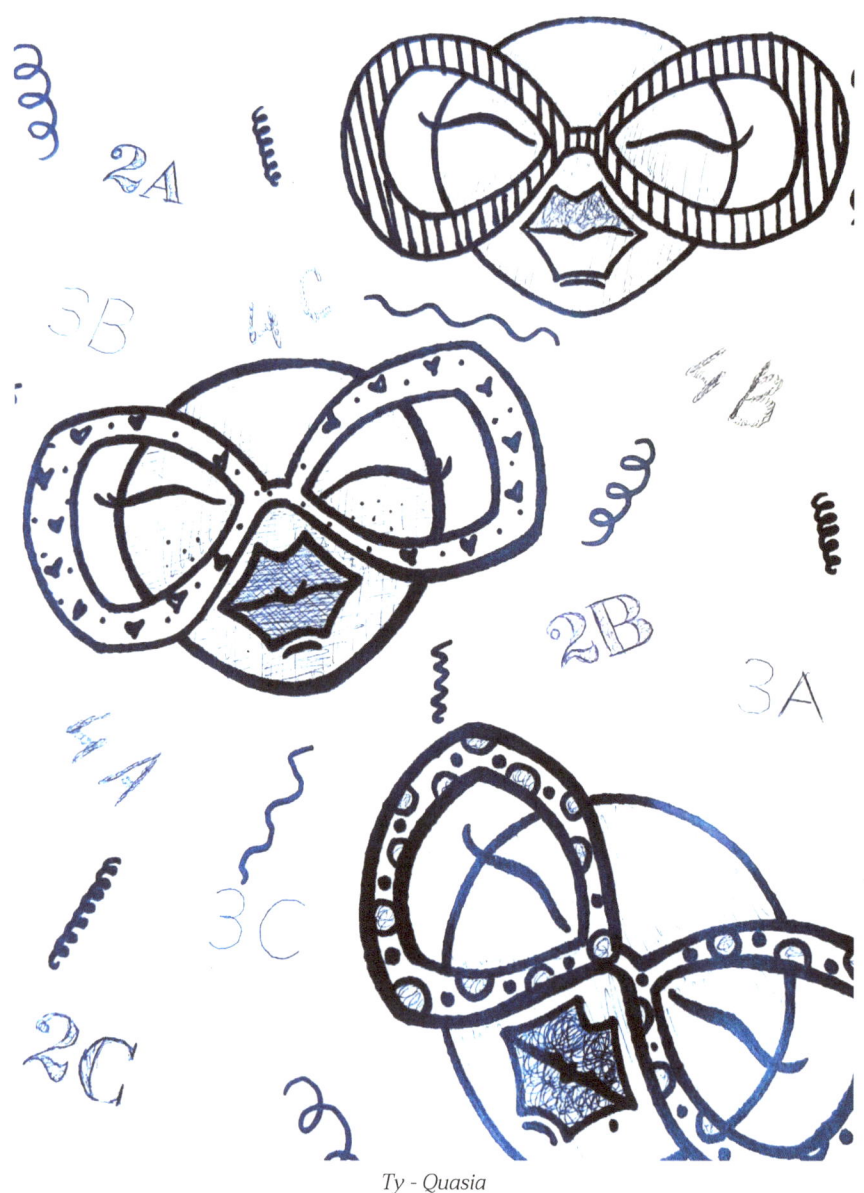

Ty - Quasia

8:32pm

I have to put a hat on
My hair is too black
Walking in daygo
Cant be seen with these naps
I see them staring
Oh how i'm not enough
I can feel their tight lips stretch till their blushed
How shameful I make you feel
Why should i even give a fuck
Yes my hair is frizzy
But oh my hair is soft
Soulful locs
Energy obtained
Letting my hair breathe
Beaming sunlight onto the black
I set free
I love me
This hair is my protection
A section
of my legendary
Identity

Pretty

I knew what I wanted
Had to be different
Of course naturally
It's gonna be different
But to say the least
I've found my peace
She's more than beauty can describe
Like being on shrooms touching the endless sky
She glows with her dark skin
Smile expresses even more what's within1
She's built different
Like a queen with gold chains
Ready to show the world just what its made
She's a beaut i can say
Her mind keeps me hugged tight to her chains
She's the one I would carry for.
The one I admire
My Pretty

Still Mirror

I can do anything
You can ask my mirror that's facts
If it's one person who will keep it a hunnid
Its that mother fucker
as still as can be
Watching me sing and Dance
just as free as I can be
Butt ass naked
Laughing and crying from the dysphoria of me
Now
that mirror in my room
as still as can be
Really
really be trying me'
Some days their like
"oh Hey LaKhai your looking swell"
And the very next hour they say
"you don't look so well"
You say a mirror is your reflection
But i'm telling y'all it can't be
It's not like I can see myself like the mirror
as still as can be
9:18pm

Do

Do it
Seriously
Just do
To answer your question
I only have one answer
Do
Awareness is loud
Actions is bond
Do it
For the next answer to your question

7/22/2017

Don't fall in love with me
For my soul is covered in dry blood
For my mind is choosing schemes back and forth
I can't decide what's what
My seed is floating between New York buildings
Cussing
Fighting
Trying to find life
I'm floating to built
Building to grow
Growing to love
But don't fall in love
I'm not good under pressure

9/4/2017

Even the moon isn't a perfect circle
What makes you think
I'm afraid
of a mother fucker who bleeds like me

12/12/2017

The only fucks given is with myself
I can't trust ignorance
I'm too oblivious

2/9/2018

Everyone always has a plan for you
They always have a thing or two
But if I listen to you
I would be you
And shit
If you ask me
I'm precisely better than you
It's not you
It's me
Literally

03/22/2018

If you can't stand to look at yourself love
Everything you look at while you're not in the mirror
Is gonna destruct
Don't look up now
Shit dont even look down
Crying while the rocks are crumbling
Won't save you now

Roots

The hard part about being a flower
Yet strongest part
Is flowers grow in place
And their surroundings changes its pace
Its like how could you still grow after all that change
Some petals may fall
But their roots in place
I give it to the flowers
I respect their living space
05/28/2019

See you later

I never like to cry when you're walking away
It's an unsettled emotion
That leads to hours of useless thoughts
Passing through nonstop
Let's make love once more
Before I
" See you later"

09/16/2016

Upside Down

They shall never see your frowns
Smile at the ignorance
They're looking for your downs

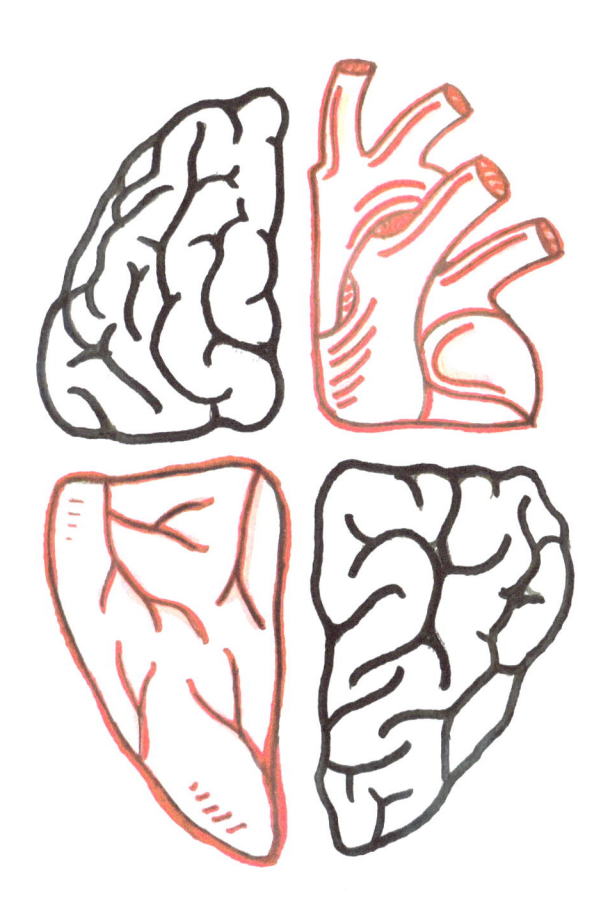

Ty - Quasi Rippey

02/2/16

She's my angel without her wings
So she can stay with me
I needed her
So God provided
She came out of nowhere
She's from the sky
A 1,000 miles away
And i couldn't imagine why
She made me stand tall
She made me see it all
I made her understand'
Thats its never gonna be another land where we stand
She my angel without her wings
Ohh how she came to me
Her smile made me fly
Her lips made me spark
Her eyes showed the light
When I crawled in the dark
She my angel without her wings
And no you can't get her things
She not allowed to leave me
My smile made her grow
My voice made her flow
She my angel without her wings
And no you can't get her things
She's not allowed to leave me
Her passion became her form
Her form was growing more
She my angel without her wings and no you can't get her things she not allowed to leave me

The devil that I am
Wants to clip them again
She's an angel with her wings
And she must be free
I'm not able to hold her

02/23/2016

They keep trying to tell me
What the fuck to do
I guess the day I listen
Is the day
I'm stuck in their shoes

06/9/2016

To find self
You must not be afraid of self
Let your body flow
Let your mouth speak
The stress your having
comes from self
And your in control
Find a cure
And be in control

BBB

A lot of pride
With a close mind
Can create destruction to self
Not acknowledging
the ignorance of the unknown
Remember
Every growth creates expanding the mind
Focus don't loose yourself
Be bigger
Better

11/10/2016

If I spit my eyes in my words
I swear you still couldn't see
Hearing the curse in my soul
Trying to find the key

02/17/2017

When I wake up
I cry for you
Then realize
What you did to me
My soul was taken
And placed nicely on a curb
So I can wake up
With a flock full of birds
My soul hurts
I can't find it
It's on the pavement somewhere off of not giving a shit

02/21/17

As much shit you did
I'm still drowning in your soul

03/31/2017

Slow burn the emotions
Let's listen to our motions
Silence create loudness
When sound gets quiet

Senseless

I don't know if my lungs are working anymore
My heart is beating
I feel it in my chest
But am I the one actually breathing
This shit can't be real
Where is the one that made it real
Forgive me
For i can't feel my heels

11/02/2017

Either i'm too small
Or too young
Or too short
Wayyyyy too nice
Or too blunt
Tell me how the fuck
Can I possibly be the best me
But never enough

11/1/2017

Insanity is knowing what to do
But being paralyzed by fear
Take me to a place
Where there's no worries
Under her arms seems so warming
But that's not gonna fix a thing

Choice

It's really what you make it
Struggle if you want
But my minds at ease

Honesty

honesty is the answer to freedom
but you don't believe me
I can tell you the HONEST fucking truth
and you speak of not seeing it
so therefore
im lying
an the loyalty is abused
degrading enhanced
do I even have a gahh damn chance
when I'm not here
I'm thinking of being there
applauding the life of honesty and love
but when I am here
I'm accused of lying
when my heart was just missing home
not knowing
the home honestly sees me as a label in the cabinets
7:30 pm

03/3/2018

Reach for the stars
But don't touch them
Their pretty to look at
But them bitches catch on fire

09/17/2018

Feeling like i'm stepping on glass
Each way up
Another soul cry tryna keep me stuck
It sucks
I can feel your heartbeat
Trying to give up
But i'm not the one to patch it up
I love you
But farewell
You can yell selfish
I'm aware

Yvonne Triche

Mantra

I choose me
Honestly and directly
Everyday in everyway
I show up for myself
Discipline over motivation
Will never be forsaken
I plant my seeds
Breathe
Take action
And choose to be happy
Everyday I learn
Everyday I grow
Everyday I prosper

Momma

I feared of being free
After the one who knows me since birth
Called me a out my frame
She doesn't know me
She just birthed me
And I had to realize That
it takes me
To show me
Once I set free
I became the flower I was made to be
And yes i'm still sprouting
Life is beautiful
Just as she
She didn't know
but
She saw me for me
after I set free
She loved me
Just how I stood
she grew herself
evolved to be
who she is today
a superwoman
nonjudgmental in anyway
And i appreciate that
Momma

8:07pm

One word text
Yeah that makes me feel good
You say you want to know me
But
One word text
makes me angry
When i try
You just
Send me something dry
Reasons why i'm distant
I feel no one can get me
But you wanna be with me
Off a
One word text

Live Nightmares

Deep sleep into an unconscious endless running of un-memorable dreams
slight movement and a quick turn
now he is woken into reality of the unknown
confused on why she's angry
telling him its no more
bubble gut from waking so instant
feeling the dislike and comfort from her
what did he do
what did he say
she won't explain
all he hears is I hate you
get out
you're a disgrace
as he take the spells from her place
soaked them up and dried them to taste
for his love is unconditional with her regardless of the space
stronger than him with much emotion
she pulls him away without any motion
his heart was pounding from heartbreak
now both of them are in a traumatic state

8:31 am

He never really spoke on things that seemed good
Always feared the things that could be
Not a risk taker
But always the person who knew
Not aware of his surroundings
Not aware he was blue
Listen to your own
It's the only way through
Another man is not God
So just Listen to you

Who is she

I Met her at a gas station
Short cut big smile
She glew of bronze beauty
She glew off her own energy
Easy to talk to
I'm in shock!
First time of me not being nervous
First time i didn't have to think
Saw her again
Shining that bronze gold
Who is she

4:04 pm

Stagnant in my sadness
I cannot have this
Is it my home
Listening for some answers
Not hearing nothing but depression
How do I unfold
Freedom of self
Is the highest of wealth
Living for self
Not someone else
I feel free
I feel like me
This is where i'm supposed to be

Reciprocate

I got 10,000 shoulders for you to cry on
But let me lean in
And fall right on my face
Look around
And your no where in place
Trust
Ha
I trust myself
I know you didn't see
but I did
just fell flat on my face

Forever Maybe

She listens to me
But hides from her
I couldn't tell you one thing about her
She says shes all about me
But really into her phone
But maybe it's insecurities that I hold
that's something on my own
I have to unfold
How can I know
I can't step back into the past
Communication is the only way
That this can last
But
You're so far away
How can I love
You're so far away
How can i really indulge
And see the person
You really are
You could be a lie
That's suppressing from a hidden scar
Or
You could be it
The one i have kids with
The one who i could be with
Forever

Spicy

She's Spicy
Like a jalapeno
Not too hot
But that flavor
Ouu that flavor a big impact
Smooth and perfect complexion
Stems right out to my perfection

Happy

I'm Happy
I am
I just feel this void from time to time
But for the most part im happy
It's a natural state
To feel within sanity
Sometimes it's the hormones
Sometimes i'm not sure
But one thing I know
I choose to remain
Tall and smile when i feel free
Because in all ends of matter
I'm happy

Chef Khonsu

He/She

He she
Oh you a boy now
I can smell your hormones
Demon ungodly
She he
He she
What ever you are
You're not safe
Around in my space
Move forward freak
Don't touch me
I might turn trans
Ew look at your feet
Why you so tall
Why her hands so big
Oh is that a she he
Or he she
How do they say it
They are disgusting
That all us Cis folks need to know
They aren't real beings
That's all we truly know
He she
Oh you a boy now
Well i'm still gonna call you her because
That's what I see

Big Little Bro

Swinging from his swinging chair
his head tilts the swing over
Fried chicken in his left hand
Fist pressured in the right
Smiling on the floor
From what's became the sight
He is a bad ass kid
Curious and motivated
Nobody could tell him about himself
A true aries you see
Grew up tall and smart
First person I ever
Told i was me
He looked at me
For quite some time
And said
I dont like gay people
Yea I guess this what they mean
when they say
Coming out the closet is a thing
Not the new fashion statement
But a whole thing
He was about 10 maybe
Young and innocent as could be
But
How could you hate
At ten
my family jokes always was a bond

But majority of their jokes had to deal with gays
Look how he walk
Look at that
We had a old man named cat across the street from grandmas
Flamboyant and free
Us as kids use to throw rocks at his house
Yelling laughing disrespecting his being
Not knowing that what we was doing wasn't just wrong but
Ignorant
examples and observation from surroundings
Really can encode your brain
It takes a being setting free
To realize that's humans are just like
You and me
My little brother never shows me hate
He stood up for me
And learned and grew
found a opinion for himself
And till this day and forever on
I just have to say
thank you for being the man you're today
you truly are a big little brother
11:48 pm

Parents

See my parents are jacks of all trades
It's a fact
Oh how I always was near
Watching them do whatever they was set to do
very logic
Nicest people you'll meet
Goofy and silly
The people you would want to be
But sometimes
they got scared
And I get it
past traumas
sometimes never heals
Sometimes we don't know our traumas
Sometimes we choose to just kneel
I use to be afraid of talking to them
out of perspective of self
and it sucks to even think
Why you dont wanna speak
But our parents
You see
Might be a reflection of thee
But they are not you
And yea
They would've known you since birth
But they are not who bring you worth
You are
So dont be afraid to tell you parents your dreams

Their learning you
In all the schemes
Find common ground
And stand yours
Show them who you are
And be bold
Respect them
Of course
They try
And its coming from the heart
My parents are great
they respect me for who I am
they are the ones I hype
"Yea my parents can do that too"
The ones who loves me no matter what
The ones who accepted me to be free

Toxic Love

I was in love once
The toxic kind
Drugs sex and drama
Felt like the world was moving just because of the word
ours
They say love is a drug
But fuck drugs
It's heartbreak
A emotion so limitless
Anything could drown you
Deeper and deeper
In the black water
Logically physically not there
A feeling of nothingness
A feeling undescribed
Toxic love is the worse
that all can be
Perspectives shifts to insanity
You now running butt ass naked in the streets
But not for freedom
But for toxic love
So the people looking at you
Don't set you free
All they see is
Anger and insecurities

Hierarchy

I feel , I feel
flustered
At my career high
One job
But miserable
But but
Its okay
Im making the money right
Even though I get headaches
From left to right
I feel I feel
Angry
I'm just not happy
But but
Its okay
Because
I'm a boss now
Right

Love Not Need

I don't love you because I need you
I love you for you
I don't want to because you want to
I want to because I do
I love myself
As you should
We can't go further
If you love me because
I love you
08/27

Factual

I see who I am
And i accept it
I actually love it
I feel free
Nothing else can stop me
But me
And since I set free
I'm willing to be a better me
And love and accept others as well
For we all are trying to not be in hell

Reminder

Mindset is everything
And i'm obsessed with my life
So
Self doubt is nothing to fear
As I overcome my trauma
I am manifesting with the universe
And i am free to all I desire
Money is an abundance
As love is happiness
It's what I choose to be
9:47 am

Placement

Took a shroom trip
Shit was mad lit
Look in the mirror and seen me
I looked like me
Talked like me
I'm right where i'm supposed to be

Her And I

Soft lips with gum drop eyes
She is my slow motion
With everything fast
Drained from all the surroundings
She is my support
Just the space
Of her and I
Makes the world
feel like it's in my palm
Not the sky
Were Meant to be
Made from rib to rib
Just had to do a little transition
To find another
Here we unfold
And become whole
Powerful to the world
Ready to take it all
Her and I
I and her

Chef Khonsu

Reality

Small smirks walking by
Their still cornering their eyes on me
They think i'm different
unique
This world likes too much blandness
lives who live and be real
They think
It's funny
Confused on how I can just be
They laugh at me
When in reality their bowing to their knees
your welcome
I get it
Now come and follow
See what being real
Can set abound to your feet

Present Presence

Present is present
If you get what I mean
Over thinking on the future
Can cause too much stress
Shoulda
Coulda
Woulda
Is all in the past
That's the gift
of the now
Nothing more to
a present to unwrap
as long as that present
was at that moment you cherished

Relax

Green feathered waves prickling my toes on this grounded grass
Kites smiling at me above my head
Left and right the trees are waving saying "hello"
So many details in a moment of space
So many wonders right at the surface of my face
It shouldn't be sadness
If the flowers sprout
It shouldn't be loneliness
If there's trees that shout
It's so many small details
We forget what's not lost
Take a moment to breathe
And let your feelings join the breeze
7:43pm

7:49 pm

There was this bumblebee
That sat right beside me
They said "you know what's black and white"
I said plenty
They said "yes but not I "
I looked down and smiled
Who do you want to be
They said very genuine
"A bumble bee silly"
Who wouldn't wanna be me?

Earth/Wind/Fire

Grounded like fire
Windy like sin
Bound to be perfection
But the fears was within
The fiery ground finally died down with the wind
And the earth is now above my feet
But the fear is still inside of me
I need to find the powers of each
earth
wind and fire
So I can balance myself
And become one

Soul Food

The soul to my food
Like smothered chicken breast with collards greens
The soul of my heart
Like fried chicken eaten from the aluminum tin
She is the soul to my veins
The feeling of pulling a wishbone
And keeping the wish to never leave
Constantly in wish
But i know the soul to my food
Will always be forever
She's my feed and thirst
The reason my eyes are always in a gaze

Four Walls

My personality is way to big for these four walls
and your control
I am way more than you want me to be
And that's okay
It's just time for me to leave
As i let one thing go another comes flourishing in
No matter what
I will win

11:56pm

I need you to guide me to think logically
I move off my heartbeat
And when she's at peak, i'm ready to take that leap
But everythings not all about feeling
Logical thinking is just as crucial
I can't keep moving off my heartbeat
She keeps leaping and not reciprocating
The pounding is slowing down
No longer hearing what beat to save
And it's got to be only one reason
I can't separate which way
Logically im not feeling
Blindsided by my own fate
I guess it's never to late
But here I am in this fucking circle again
Lost and unsettled
Heartbroken from the broken record
Why can't I
Just accept and move from this test
Set free and burn out of this flesh
Then at that point
I can really
Really balance myself

94 ~ BY CHEF KHONSU

Ty - Quasia Rippey

Self Made Prison

I can feel my heart on a hold
Not trying to let go
And i see it when I look in her eyes
Shes loves me but cant get to me
I'm behind these bars trying to reach
But in order for me to unlock these doors
I must let go and choose to freely be me
These bars are made with trauma and insecurities
Heartbreak and devastation
The keys are RIGHT HERE in my pocket
Out of my reach
I must sit and meditate
Sit and think
But here she is
five feet from me
Wondering why i'm struggling to breathe
12:54am

Chained Loose

I know who I am
I do
I swear
This choke hold on me
is just you know
chained
It's there
I didn't make it
You people did
I didn't ask for this
You tried to chain me
You tried to make me something I wasn't
And now every so then
I second guess myself
But
I know who I am

1:28 pm

Skeptical on what to do
She likes him
But events are appearing
Making him not look like what she sees
Makes sense
She just met him
But what can the man do
If all odds are bounding to be untruth
What can he feel
If the love of his life
Doesn't feel it's real
Only thing is to build trust
And that takes time
So i hope she's ready for the ride

First Off

She instantly responded
As if she knew we both was up to no good
What do you do when chemistry attracts
But friendship lacks
I'm hurt and I can't relax
Honesty is my best form
And I dont think i'm ready
because
Hurt people hurt people
You can't come and save me
It's my own thing
Saying you love me won't change a thing
Loving myself first
Then maybe we can become a thing

Space

Hold me down
And control my life
I don't think so
Only I can decide
Whats my next jive
And you're not going to control it
They say get a job work your way up
But some people
That ain't the case
Personality too big
Energy too independent
I want my own space

Circle Back

Its that loving I crave
Longing for you because
You're so far away
Flashbacks of memories
When you were inside of me
Flashbacks of our eye contact
As my heavy breathe aggressively paints
And rolls my eyes back
Sensitive and lost in arousal
I without hesitant spread open more
Now she's deeper and i'm lusting for more
Then she pulls me
Grasping my climax
I release
It's the smell of you and I
Now lingering the air
Passionate and in love
Lets circle back
And do once more
Star at midnight
Star at midnight
Oh how urge for you in daylight
I chase you at the top of the climax
to grab mid air
you're not there
I'm Gasping for air
Unfolding dust
Making dust my shield
So close

Yet so far
I go to reach
And you kill me with flames
Burn my flesh
Yet purify my veins
I'll smile under the moonlight in amaze
The most beautiful things aren't reached
The most horrible things are felt
How can my star be in this battle of concept
My star at midnight
Oh how i urge for you in the day

T for Tea

I can show you the ways
on why I love you
Sit
and let me explain
Let's have a cup of tea
For this is Tea for T
Take a seat with me
Green eyes on most days
Brown on others
Somethings only you and I will understand
It's not the color I glare into
but the indents of how your gum drop eyes curve
And the lines on your eyelids
Telling me some stories
You haven't showed
She trying to cover her smile
Your smile is something God said
lay wisdom and beauty on her lips
It's the way you walk with confidence
The way your lips touch mine
I can show you the ways on why
I love you
Come here
take a seat
Lets have some tea
God sat with me once before
And said
You will fall in love with a woman

The woman you've been asking me for
Her eyes will unlock your home
And her mind will keep you stern
And together you will become one
But it takes more then just love
I just didn't .. I didn't
know what he meant
I thought being in love was just that
He said
Time goes at a weird space
And in that weird time it's in between the lines
And in order to understand and to prepare
And to be ready to know who this person is
I need you to open your eyes and meditate
You need to know the difference of what's love and what's
not
She's a strong woman who will have your heart but not just
that
Your soul
She will shoot the layers of stubborness from your skin
And gently come in
She is your forever
And the next time you pour a cup of tea
It's not gonna be with me
It's going to be different
New
Perfect for you
T for Tea is a hint
But self understanding is the key
I can tell you many ways
How
Why
I love you
Dark skin

Eyebrows always on ten
Tall and crisp
Like a portrait in a mansion
But you see
It's not your physical appearance that i've fallen in love with
It's the value
the gentleness
The boldness
The spice of her seasoning that marinates into mine
That created this chemistry
That I just I just
Cannot decline
Oh how I love you
And how I know when
God said to me
You will fall in love with a woman
the one you been asking
You were her
Sit her down
Make some tea
Show her the details of me
As she showed me the details of you
Our God together
We are one
One rib for you the other for her
In order for her to connect to you
You both must
Open up and be free with each other
to be relieved from others
And be
I can say darling
I can Tell you many ways on why I love you
Like how I say I want to cater you for a spa day and you say

What about you
Or how you talk so Godly and how you talk so fierce
How you lay your hands on my chest and hold your hand on my heart
While I feel you pulse in my skin
I will kiss your scars in this lifetime
And the next
I will take off all my clothes and open my closet
And my chest
So you will completely be into me
Inside me as a whole
As I seen you step into my closest with all my clothes and bones
I thought I thought
My body would be shaking due to the nakedness in the cold
Instead it was warm like hot coffee when we wake up
And toasty like that burnt cheesy bread you adore so much
At first i was shy and surprise you just appeared and showed up
And my mistake was second guessing what God had roasted in his crockpot
For me
You're perfect just like this cup of tea
And i wanted to sit you down
So to explain
God has definitely sent you my way.

10:09 am

On the outside i'm composed
Internally i'm trying to control
my anxiety
Setting free of me
But human stupidity keeps lingering
Not allowing me to breathe
and make excuses
To be victim
And not cut loose of
what is
surrounding my souls truth

Just Me

I remember
childhood days back
Having a TV show with my mirror
I turned the shower on
And sung my intro
It was called the Kai'la show
I did stand up
I danced
I even had and emotional part where I mention unstable
beings in their chaos
Like i knew what that was at 12
Now
I keep hearing that i'm the same person
since I became a man
As if i took a needle to my ass to be a whole new person
Like God said this Testerone will kill you
Put you in the same body
but different mind
You're not you
What point would that make
Just kill me and place me in a different realm
For that sake
shooting myself in my ass
to be someone else
Sounds absurd
You all are overthinking this
It's just me

Break

Now that we need a break
I feel you so much stronger
Not in a passionate way
But intense
A break from someone whose flaws make me smirk
A break from someone who just came up and stole my heart
What the fuck is a break
And how can my mind even stay calm
I'm trying to give you space
But now this break making me feel you don't want our love
In a way
I can't move right now
I don't know what to do
I'm forcing myself to do some push ups
Forcing myself to give you room
My heart has sunken to my feet
And my feet can't even think of which way to fleet
Help me God for i know I shouldn't worry
I know my heart is with hers and i know im trustworthy
I know she feeling many ways
And the best way to support her
is to respect her wish

Pointy Heart

I like drawing sharp hearts
pointy edges
black scribble lines
filling the inside
slightly crooked on the canvas of space
to me a sharp heart shows the truth
three pin points
trust
comfort
and individuality
imagine your sharp heart next to your soul expressing the
true feeling of love
sharp pinching the muscle to blood stream
being the days where it just hurts
that scribbled ink filling the empty spaces that needed to
be
small white spaces where the ink missed providing self
views of the unknown
finding the unknown to be marked with black
balancing against the soul trying to find the perfect
crooked angle
I like pointy hearts
it shows the truth of love
the pain of love

nothing is perfect like those soft fluffed up hearts
perfectly fit on the canvas
love takes sharp corners
filling tiny spaces
that are quite huge
most ask what is love
and most answer with lies
I can describe to you the beauty
but I also need to describe all the true feelings
so first
lets start by drawing a pointy heart

KAI'LA LAKHAI ~ 111

Tyson Marzouq

Kai'la LaKhai

Since life became meaningful
I knew something was off
I remember sitting in the passenger seat in my moms car
Hand on my chin staring out the window
I'm alive
But somethings not right
Mirror searching
I'm beautiful but
Somethings not right
I opened my canvas right outside the park
Opening the skeletons and overused heart
Gushing out like a swarm of flies
Insecurities everywhere
There's no hidden space to hide
Kai'la whats wrong whats setting us apart
I move from land to land looking for the correction
Finally landed with a transman who said the words I was
looking for
And then
Kai'la Became LaKhai
And LaKhai was ready to take over the temple
Chest
Voice
Hair
and all
LaKhai dug and dug inside their temple
Doing what Kai'la asked him to
Bury her , let her die

Give her no space to be able to be vulnerable again
Lock up her kindness so we dont get fucked over again
Shut her mouth so no one can hear her speak anymore
Digging and digging
years go by
And LaKhai was circling and circling in his temple
Not understanding the absence
What is this absence
I've done everything I can do
To be me
Circling and circling
LaKhai decides to take a new turn
And stumble on the patch he patched
Written old soul
If my soul is one
Should my body be too?
He dug and dug
And Resurfaced Kai'la
And life at that moment
Became full

Chef Khonsu

Chef Khonsu: Culinary Innovator, Writer, and Advocate for Well-being

As a culinary magician and captivating storyteller, Chef Khonsu has dedicated his life to spreading positivity and joy through his culinary creations and heartfelt narratives. Raised in a military family, Chef Khonsu explored diverse cultures across the United States, enriching his palette and understanding of global cuisines. His journey of self-discovery led him to the practices of meditation and manifestation, which have deeply influenced his culinary and personal philosophy.

Chef Khonsu's passion for food and writing linked to his mission of promoting self-love, growth, and holistic well-being. With a keen interest in the study of spices and herbs, he emphasizes the importance of life transitions and mental health, aiming to nourish both the mind and the stomach.

In 2016, Chef Khonsu founded Ktfood-ies, a venture that evolved into Goldjestic in 2023. This rebranding marked the expansion of his business into a multifaceted entity that encompasses culinary innovation, education, and advocacy. His diverse interests, including sports, music, and dancing, further enhance his creative approach to his work.

Chef Khonsu's brand, Goldjestic, stands as a testament to his commitment to delivering exceptional culinary experiences while fostering a community centered on self-improvement and holistic health.

- Culinary Expertise: Mastery in blending diverse cultural influences and studying the therapeutic properties of spices and herbs.
- Holistic Advocate: Promotes mental health awareness and personal growth through culinary arts and storytelling.
- Entrepreneurial Leadership: Successfully rebranded and expanded his business from Ktfood-ies to Goldjestic, reflecting a broader and more integrated approach to his mission.
- Creative Pursuits: Engages in various creative outlets, including music and dancing, which contribute to his dynamic and innovative style.

Chef Khonsu's unique blend of culinary skills, educational initiatives, and advocacy for well-being makes him a distinguished figure in the culinary world. Connect with Chef Khonsu to explore collaborations, culinary innovations, and initiatives that aim to enrich lives through the power of food and positive storytelling.

As He always says
"Khai is Khai, and you are you."

Milton Keynes UK
Ingram Content Group UK Ltd.
UKHW051039021024
449153UK00003B/22